VASCO DA GAMA
Sailor Toward The Sunrise

Vasco da Gama

SAILOR TOWARD THE SUNRISE

By RONALD SYME

Illustrated by WILLIAM STOBBS

WILLIAM MORROW AND COMPANY

New York 1959

Published simultaneously in the Dominion of Canada
by George J. McLeod Limited, Toronto. Printed in the
United States of America.
Library of Congress Catalog Card No. 59-5018

••••••••••

Also by Ronald Syme

CARTIER, FINDER OF THE ST. LAWRENCE
DE SOTO, FINDER OF THE MISSISSIPPI
BALBOA, FINDER OF THE PACIFIC
HENRY HUDSON
JOHN SMITH OF VIRGINIA
MAGELLAN, FIRST AROUND THE WORLD
LA SALLE OF THE MISSISSIPPI
COLUMBUS, FINDER OF THE NEW WORLD
CHAMPLAIN OF THE ST. LAWRENCE
CORTES OF MEXICO
All Illustrated by William Stobbs

BAY OF THE NORTH
Illustrated by Ralph Ray

Ten-year-old Vasco da Gama was sitting quietly on the warm sand, his shoulders resting against the tarred black side of a fishing boat. The hot sunshine of Portugal sparkled on the nearby sea. Behind him stood the red-tiled houses of the village called Sines, and beyond the houses dark pine forests rose on the distant hills. At one end of the bay there was a high, gray-walled castle on a headland covered with yellow-flowered gorse. Long white fishing nets were drying on high wooden frames. In the distance a black-hulled little ship was spreading her white canvas sails and gliding away with the morning tide.

Vasco's home was at Sines. He knew the village so well that he never troubled to look at the castle, or the gorse, or the coils of fishing line in the boats. Vasco was more interested in unusual sights, and so he was watching the little ship gliding into the distance. The vessel reminded him of the story of Prince Henry the Navigator, a story he had learned at school. Indeed, the prince, who had died in 1460, the year Vasco was born, was a hero to every Portuguese boy.

Perhaps that ship is going to Africa, Vasco thought to himself. She'll bring back gold and pepper, white rhinoceros ivory and Negro slaves.

It was Prince Henry who had sent the first ships down the west coast of Africa years and years ago. He wanted them to find a way around the unknown end of the continent, so that they might be able to sail onward to that strange country called India.

The prince had taken the best map makers, astronomers, and navigators in Portugal to live with him in a castle overlooking the sea. "We know that Arab vessels already bring rich cargoes from India to Arabia," he told them. "Camel caravans take the cargoes across the Arabian Desert to the wealthy merchants of Venice and Genoa. Those two cities have grown rich on their imports of silks and spices, diamonds, perfumes, and gold from India. Our own vessels could bring back similar cargoes to Portugal. And so we must send vessels to find a route around the southern end of Africa."

The prince and his wise men never succeeded. Their mariners reached Cape Verde, on a barren stretch of sea, and found nothing but black savages, a red-hot wind roaring off the desert, and sharks as big as a Portuguese fishing boat. The vessels crept on down past Cape Verde and round the big western bulge of Africa. Their captains drew careful charts of the coast and brought them back to Prince Henry.

"Good, but not yet far enough," the Navigator said to them. "Sail again and try to go still farther south. One day you will reach the southern tip of Africa."

There was always difficulty in finding sailors to man the ships for these expeditions. Seafarers—and everyone else, for that matter—believed that frightful monsters lived in the deep oceans. It was said that there were whales big enough to swallow a ship, and sea serpents with heads as big as a barrel and slimy bodies as long as the beach at Sines. And yet, somehow, the sailors were found. Prince Henry's vessels went on exploring farther and farther

south. But the prince died with his great quest unfinished. No one had yet reached the southern end of Africa and the sea route to India.

Perhaps there isn't such a route, Vasco thought to himself. He was a dark-haired, sturdy, obstinate boy, who preferred solid facts to dreams. His father was one of the king's officers, and his grandfather had been a good, steady-going soldier. The da Gama family seldom wasted time on idle thoughts and fancies. There was English blood in their veins, and it made them a cold and practical people. Vasco was quite sensible enough to realize that Portugal was becoming wealthy on her imports from west Africa. It was Prince Henry who had found the road to that wealth, and he had done Portugal a great service. But perhaps he was wrong in declaring that there was a sea route to India.

The years went by, and Vasco forgot the day he had sat on the beach as a ten-year-old boy to watch a vessel sail for an unknown destination. But he did not forget that Prince Henry had said there was a sea route to India. No one knew yet if the Navigator was right or wrong.

At the age of fifteen, Vasco became a sailor. He voyaged down to Africa in order to see the continent with his own eyes. He came to know the heat and fury of sandstorms roaring seaward off the Sahara Desert. Mud-walled villages, strange animals, and savage Negro tribes became familiar sights to him. In time he learned to navigate his own ship through wild tempests of tropical rain and to come safely to anchor through the warm white fogs rolling off coastal mangrove swamps.

Captain Vasco da Gama was a silent and fierce-tempered young man, but he was honest with the merchants who engaged him to sail their ships. The men who formed his crew found that they had a harsh but fair-minded commander. Gama never cared to talk about his adventures on the Guinea Coast, as west Africa was called in those days. He took his ship out and back, submitted his report to the owners, but never wrote a word more than he had to. No one today knows just where Gama sailed or how far southward he went.

Meanwhile, in the year 1488, when Gama was twenty-eight years old, an exploring Portuguese sea captain named Bartholomew Diaz was unexpectedly swept, with his three little ships, round the southern end of Africa. This accidental discovery of the sea route to India was a terrifying experience. The ships were tiny and the cold seas more mountainous and destructive than those of the Guinea Coast. The frightened Portuguese seamen believed that they were very near death. When they heard that Captain Diaz was now thinking of trying to sail onward to India, they mutinied against him.

"Let the saints bear witness that we have done enough," they grumbled to Diaz. "We have charted nearly two thousand miles of unknown coast and have at last found the sea passage round the end of the Dark Continent. This is great and good news for us to carry back to King John of Portugal. Should we go farther now, we might die of thirst and hunger. News of our discovery will never reach Portugal if we are lost at sea. Is it not enough that we must now sail back around that high and frightful headland you rightly named the Stormy Cape?"

Poor Bartholomew Diaz was forced to turn back. And so he may very well have lost the honor of being the first European to reach India by sea. He reached Portugal at the end of 1488 and told his story to the king.

The sea route to the wealth of India now lay open to the ships of Portugal. But for nearly ten years King John hesitated to dispatch a vessel to make the voyage. Meanwhile, the Spanish vessels of Columbus had discovered the American continent, and Spaniards were pouring across the Atlantic to the islands of the Caribbean Sea.

One reason for the king's delay was that it was difficult to find men willing to make the voyage. Portuguese seamen were scared at the thought of going around the Cape of Good Hope, as King John had named Diaz's Stormy Cape, and sailing onward for thousands of miles to unknown India. "Diaz was lucky," they said. "He sailed through monstrous storms and lost only one ship. But men might drown or starve or die of thirst if they tried to go the whole enormous distance to India."

There were other reasons for King John's delay. Mighty Spain, disappointed at finding so little gold in the West Indies, was becoming jealous of Portugal. The sultan of Egypt and the rulers of the powerful city of Venice were angry at the thought of Portugal's interfering with their prosperous trade with India.

"If all our enemies combine against us," the king's advisers said, "Portugal will be destroyed. It would be wiser to be satisfied with our profitable trade with west Africa and leave India alone."

Early in the year 1495, King John realized that death was reaching out for him. He was only forty years old, but he had many enemies in Portugal. People whispered that he was being secretly poisoned by the families of certain nobility whom he had either wrongfully imprisoned or put to death.

King John may have been a villain at heart, but he had the high courage of an explorer. While in the great council chamber of his palace one day, he happened to glance up from some documents on the table in front of him. Passing through the room was a short, burly, hard-featured young man, whose

bearded face was tanned by the winds and the tropical sun.

"Friend Vasco da Gama!" King John exclaimed. "I know you as one of the best sea captains of Portugal. There will be a fine expedition for you to lead before very long, for I have decided to send ships to India."

King John did not live to see his expedition sail from Lisbon. He died a few months after he had chosen Vasco da Gama as commander.

But John's cousin, Manuel, who then became king, went ahead with the idea. He found the money for the voyage and ordered the ships to be built. Manuel asked Bartholomew Diaz to advise Gama on the building of these ships.

"We've had the wrong idea in the past," Diaz told Gama. "Our ships' decks curve too much, and those high wooden castles we've been building at bow and stern are all wrong. They're useful for defense when an enemy boards the ship, but they create too much weight. When you hit those wild seas around the Cape of Good Hope, you should have level decks and not too much weight above the water line. Low-built ships with deep hulls are what you'll need.

"And here's something else, friend Vasco. For the past seventy-five years our ships have always steered along the African coast when they voyaged south. Winds and currents are against them all the way. I found that out for myself when I got far south. So I advise you, my good friend, to steer well out into the Atlantic until you reach twenty degrees south of the equator. Then swing eastward, and I've an idea—it's just an idea, mind you—that you'll go tearing in toward the Cape of Good Hope with a singing breeze to tighten your sails. It's what I'd do if King John—God rest his soul—had chosen me as leader instead of you.

"One more thing. Watch your men for mutiny. If my own hadn't rebelled, I might have reached India seven years ago. But the men would sail no farther, and I gave way to them. Maybe that's why our present king—may his reign be happy and prosperous—didn't choose for me to go with you."

Three little ships arose on the wooden slipways beside Lisbon's wide Tagus River. All of them were three-masters. There was the *Sao Gabriel,* the flagship, which weighed about 240

tons; the *Sao Rafael,* about 200 tons; and the *Sao Maria,* about 150 tons. A fourth vessel, the *Berrio,* was bought from a Portuguese sea captain. She was a two-masted little vessel of 100 tons, fitted with triangular fore-and-aft sails, like those of a modern yacht.

Veteran seamen scratched their heads and wondered greatly when they looked at the three new ships. They were reasonably high at bow and stern, but their decks were

strangely level. Foremasts and mainmasts carried square sails, but the mizzenmasts—those nearest the stern—were fitted with triangular sails. On each mast was a lofty crow's-nest for lookouts. The decks were fitted with clumsy iron guns, and a good deal of space was occupied by heavy boats.

"Flatter-bottomed than most and fitted with those newfangled watertight compartments," muttered the seamen. "They're queer-looking vessels, but Captain Diaz designed them and Captain da Gama approved of the design. Between them there isn't much they don't know about seamanship. Even so, no vessels like those yonder have ever yet sailed out of Portugal."

The completed vessels were moored beside the wharves of Lisbon. Into their holds were swung barrels of salt beef and pork; barrels of wine; cases of lentils, sardines, plums, onions, honey; bags of salt and sugar; and casks of brandy. There were other barrels containing gunpowder, and coils of flax rope, spare anchors, sails, steel breastplates, crossbows, and bundles of clothing. The voyage might last three years, and Gama had no intention of running short of supplies.

There was only one important item which Gama apparently overlooked—or perhaps did not bother to include. He took no supplies of costly presents for the native princes he might meet during the journey. Gama was accustomed to dealing with the simple Negroes of west Africa. He had a rather superior attitude toward colored races, and he believed any kind of trash was good enough for them, as long as it was made in Europe. This mistake was to cause endless trouble.

While the vessels were being loaded and the hatches fastened down, Gama went searching for crews to man his vessels. He chose his older brother, Paulo, to be captain of the 200-ton *Sao Rafael.* Paulo was a lean, gentle-voiced man with a generous heart. Behind his polite manners and soft voice, however, there dwelt a fierce temper and unlimited courage. In addition, he was a first-class seaman.

One by one, men came forward. They were already scared at the thought of the coming voyage into strange and unknown seas. Apart from the gentlemen who volunteered merely for the sake of adventure, there were some

strange characters. Martin Affonso, seaman, had lived for years among the Negro tribes of west Africa and spoke their queer, clicking language. Joao Nunes, sailmaker, had wandered through Arabia and spoke Hebrew and Arabic. Pero Aguilar, clerk, was an ugly little man and handy with a knife. Some said he was a fugitive from Spain. Fernao Martins spoke Arabic but was careful not to reveal how and where he had learned that language.

Juan de Acaray, quartermaster, was a Spaniard and a deadly shot with a crossbow.

Gama also enlisted twelve convicts who had been condemned to long imprisonment or death. During the voyage they were to be put ashore, if necessary, to search for food and water, to look for signs of treachery among the natives, and to make friends with tribes who appeared hostile. Provided these men behaved themselves—and lived long enough—they were to receive a pardon for their crimes. Altogether, Vasco da Gama collected about 150 men for his ships.

On July 8, 1497, the four vessels moved a mile or two downstream from the city of Lisbon. They anchored in a reach where the river ran wide and deep. Cool orchards and bright gardens covered the banks. On the summit of the low hills, windmills spun briskly in a warm breeze. The sun was bright in a cloudless summer sky, and the blue surface of the Tagus River was covered with sparkling wavelets.

The four vessels looked trim and efficient. Gay flags and pennons were flying from the masts; the freshly-painted hulls glistened in the sunlight. On each white sail was painted a large red cross. The officers and the gentlemen on deck were wearing new cloaks and uniforms, and the ships glowed with their bright colors.

A great crowd had gathered on the grassy banks to say farewell to the men who now came ashore for the last time. Highborn ladies with scarlet flowers in their black hair stood next to handsome peasant women who wore colored silk scarves knotted loosely round their shoulders. Shepherds, cowherds, and farmers, in homespun clothing, gazed with wonder—and perhaps with envy, too—at the splendid little vessels and the brown-skinned sailors in their red tasseled caps. There were dark-skinned gypsy girls; gray-haired, wrinkled seamen who had sailed in the vessels sent out by Prince Henry the Navigator forty years earlier; and pale-faced priests in garments of black.

Watching this bright yet sorrowful scene—for many in the crowd were weeping—was Vasco da Gama. He was leaning on the poop rail of the *Sao Gabriel,* a thickset, heavy-shouldered, strong-jawed man, thirty-seven years old. Sailors on the deck below cast inquisitive glances up at him. They noticed his dark, watchful eyes, his powerful arms, and the hard line of his mouth.

"Not a man to rouse to anger," muttered a seaman. "I've heard stories about what he's like in a temper. A devil spitting fire, so they say!"

"Aye," murmured another, "but he's surely the best man to lead us to this distant land of India. He's never lost a ship in all his years at sea, or known a mutiny either. He'll give jus-

tice to those who obey his orders, whatever he may do to the others."

The seamen were right. Years spent in the slave trade of west Africa had turned Captain Vasco da Gama into a hard and sometimes ruthless man. Nothing and no one were allowed to stand in his way. While the crowd on shore wept as they embraced their departing husbands, fathers, and sons, Gama's bearded face remained grim and without emotion. The greatest voyage of his life was about to begin. The king of Portugal had entrusted the expedition to him. Success meant wealth for the country; failure would bring disgrace on the family name of Gama. There must be no mistakes on this voyage, and no rebellious crews to threaten mutiny because of fear.

The breeze was coming from the east. It would carry the ships down the river and into the Atlantic Ocean. Gama issued the order for trumpets to sound. The seamen rowed back aboard their vessels. Then, as the sound of weeping rose more loudly from the shore, anchors began to rise from the river mud. The white sails with the bright red crosses swelled outward from the masts. One by one, the *Sao Gabriel* leading, the little fleet began to glide down the Tagus River. The long and dangerous voyage to India had begun. This was to be the greatest day in Portugal's history.

Past low shores of sandbanks the ships steered down the west African coast. In those days ships were not fitted with water tanks below deck. Fresh water had to be carried in barrels, and there was never enough of it for a long voyage. Gama swung his ships to an anchorage in the Cape Verde Islands, where the casks were refilled. Sailors chopped great quantities of wood for the cooking stoves aboard their ships, and gathered all the fresh food they could find.

Venice
Genoa
SPAIN
PORTUGAL
Lisbon
North Atlantic Ocean
Mediterranean
30°–
Morocco
EG
Sahara Desert
15°–
Cape Verde
AFRICA
0°– EQUATOR
South Atlantic Ocean
15°–
30°–
Cape of
Good H

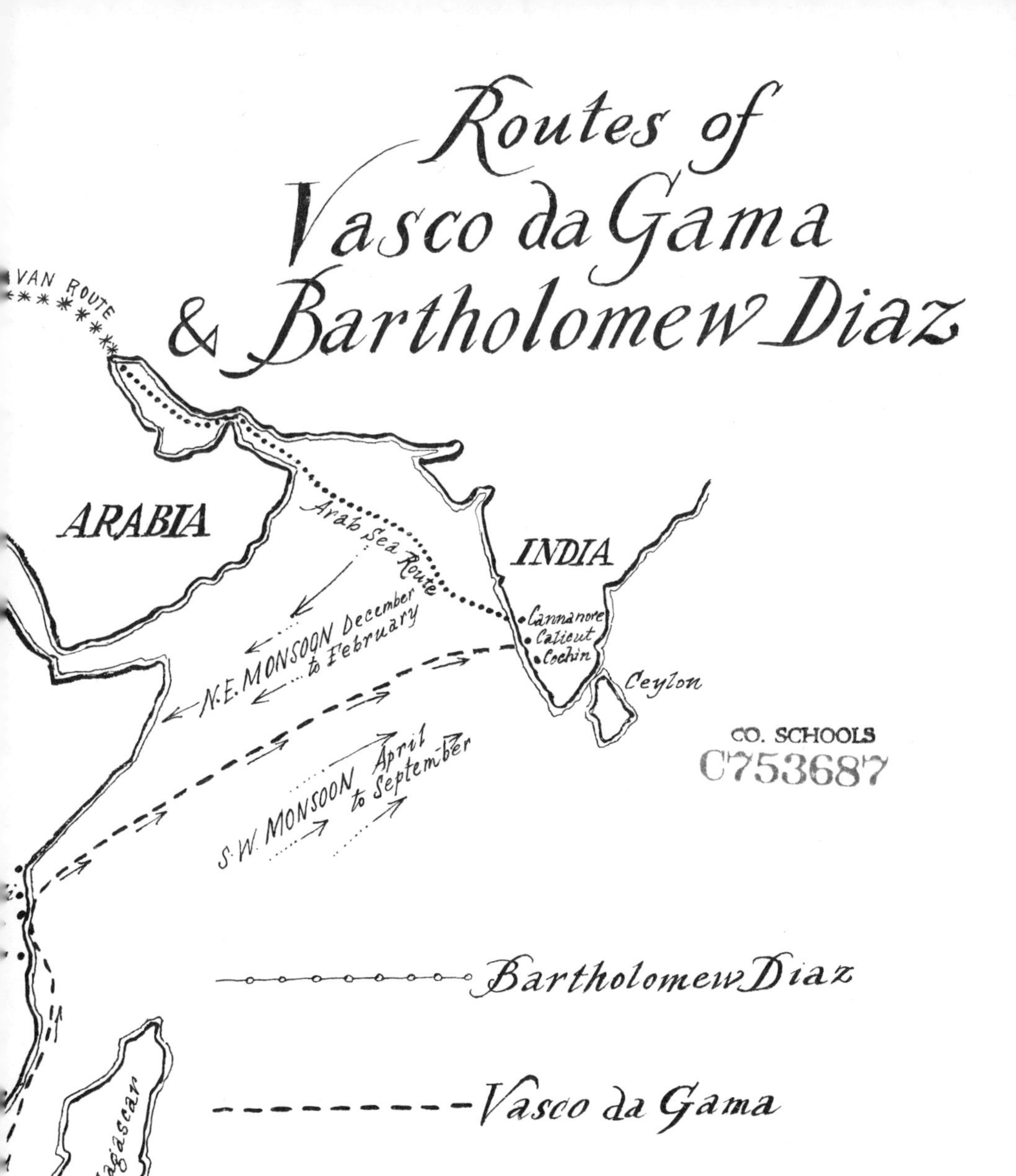
Routes of
Vasco da Gama
& Bartholomew Diaz
VAN ROUTE
ARABIA
Arab Sea Route
N.E. MONSOON December to February
INDIA
Cannanore
Calicut
Cochin
Ceylon
S.W. MONSOON April to September
Madagascar
Bartholomew Diaz
Vasco da Gama
Arab Sea Route

Far south of the Cape Verde Islands, Gama gave a surprising order to his officers. "Steer southwest," he commanded. "We are leaving the coast. There'll be many thousands of miles of open sea for us to cover before we sight land again."

Outward to the great Atlantic swung the heavy little ships. Day after day there was only the ocean around them, where great-winged albatrosses swung and dipped between the gray, hissing wave tops. The southeast trade wind blew steadily on the port quarter. Progress was slow, but not as slow as it would have been had the vessels kept to the coast on their southward run.

At twenty degrees south of the equator, Gama, following the suggestion Bartholomew Diaz had made, altered course again. "South-southeast," he ordered. "We'll swing in to the coast."

Now a westerly wind filled the great white

sails and sent the four ships pounding along to far-off Africa. August went by, and then September.

"We'll sight land in three weeks' time," said Gama, and he was right. On November 1, 1497, the three ships came tearing into St. Helena Bay, about 150 miles north of the Cape of Good Hope.

Gama had done his navigation with a sand-glass and a primitive compass. His only chart was the rough one drawn by Diaz, and he used a clumsy astrolabe instead of the modern sextant to find his latitudes. It is no wonder that his navigation is still described by seafarers today as one of the finest pieces of pure navigation ever accomplished. The course he steered was used ever afterward by sailing ships bound for South Africa.

Around the Cape of Good Hope went Gama with his ships. They called at lonely bays inhabited by Negro tribes, where they bought

fat oxen in exchange for pewter bracelets or little copper bells, and refilled the empty water casks. Portuguese seamen ate porridgelike millet and roast chicken from wooden platters in mud-walled village huts. Good-natured Negroes helped them roll the water barrels down to the boats, and afterwards sang and danced to the thin piping of native flutes.

Exploring Portuguese seamen in those days used to erect stone pillars at easily noticed places along the coast. These *padraos,* as they were called, served as guides for other ships. Each *padrao* was a circular stone column, topped by a square block of stone, upon which stood a heavy little stone cross, fixed in place with lead. On December 16, 1497, Gama left behind the last *padrao* erected by Bartholomew Diaz. His ships had reached water never seen before by any European sailor.

As the vessels crept northward up the coast of east Africa, an illness called scurvy made its terrifying appearance among the men. The disease was caused by the lack of certain vitamins found in fresh fruits and vegetables, which were almost entirely absent from a seaman's diet. Men's gums turned black, and their teeth fell out. Their legs and arms swelled most painfully, and their flesh rotted. They grew weaker day by day. Some of them died in their bunks, loudly cursing the day they had signed on for this voyage or weeping

sadly for the sweet countryside of Portugal they would never see again.

With their crews of sick and dying men, the four ships found their way into the wide, low-lying harbor of Mozambique. The surrounding hillsides were covered with green jungle, where monkeys and bright-feathered parrots chattered and squawked from dawn to sunset. On the foreshore stood white-walled houses with dome-topped windows, heavy

carved doors, and verandas with iron lattice-work.

Mozambique was an Arab town. Fierce Arab warriors, sweeping down from the north, had settled there centuries before. Their descendants had built fine houses and established trading stores. They had bought African ivory, gold, and slaves, which they exported to India in exchange for spices, carpets, and rare silks. These Arabs had grown prosperous from their

trade across the Indian Ocean. Their nation was hostile to all Christian races, so it was scarcely surprising that the Arabs in Mozambique were suspicious of the Portuguese.

Lean-faced, light-skinned men, wearing silken turbans and flowing robes of white cotton, gazed warily at the oncoming ships. The ruler of Mozambique came aboard the *Sao Gabriel* as soon as the flagship dropped anchor. He arrived in a fine large canoe, reclining on silken cushions placed on the carpet-covered deck. He was a dark, handsome man, wearing a short velvet jacket, a long blue cloak, and baggy white trousers secured tightly at his ankles. A blue silk sash encircled his waist, and from it protruded the silver-mounted handle of a dagger.

Gama sent for Fernao Martins, the man who spoke Arabic. "We are sailing onward to India," Gama told the Arab ruler through his interpreter. "I ask you to find for us a good pilot who knows the course to steer across the Indian Ocean."

"The matter might be arranged," the Arab said politely.

He paused and looked around in an expectant manner. Fernao Martins explained to Gama that on such occasions it was customary to give the prince a present. The Arab was awaiting his gift.

Gama presented this wealthy and finely

dressed Arab with a cheap red cloak, a few felt hats, a couple of shoddy linen shirts, and some coral-bead necklaces! These poor gifts put an end to any possibility of friendship between the Portuguese and the people of Mozambique. The Arab abruptly returned to the shore. Gama, realizing that trouble might start, hastily bought fresh coconuts, melons, and cucumbers from the boats which clustered round his ships. Once again he sent a party of men ashore to refill the water barrels.

Arabs attacked the seamen rolling the barrels up the beach to a nearby spring. Confronted by the angry, shouting warriors, the Portuguese retreated hastily and rowed back to their ships.

"We must have water," Gama said angrily. "Send the boats tomorrow and arm them with bombards. These Moors must be made to understand that we are now the masters here."

A fight started on the beach the following

morning. The Arabs came down to the water's edge, waving swords and barbed stabbing spears. Three bombards fired, one after the other. These portable guns were noisy and inefficient weapons, but there was no defense against their half-pound iron shot. Many Arabs dropped on the beach, and the rest fled into the jungle. Sweating Portuguese seamen hastily trundled the refilled water barrels back to the waiting boats.

Gama had reached Mozambique on March 2, 1498. His ships remained there until March 31, for northerly winds and ocean currents prevented them from leaving. He spent the entire month squabbling and skirmishing with the Arab population. The Arabs were difficult people, it was true, but Gama's violent temper was to blame for much of the trouble. He was proud and obstinate, and he was a dangerous man to deal with. When his ships finally sailed from Mozambique, he opened

fire on the town with falconets and rabinets. These were light deck guns made of brass, and their one-pound shot probably caused little serious damage to the houses ashore. Yet this final action of Gama's earned for the Portuguese the undying hatred of the Arab population of east Africa. Good seaman though he was, Gama—like most Portuguese—had no idea about how to make friends with native races.

The ships sailed northward for another week. They steered alongside a low shore covered with jungle, where lions could be heard roaring at night. On the eighth day they reached Mombasa, the finest and largest harbor on the east African coast.

The Arabs had settled in Mombasa several hundred years earlier. They had built a white-walled town with narrow, winding streets and gardens filled with tropical flowers. There

were high and graceful minarets and temples with silver-studded doors. Atop the flat-roofed buildings of the town, men and women now gathered to gaze angrily at the four approaching vessels.

The sultan of Mombasa had already heard that Gama was coming up the coast. Runners may have brought the news to him, or perhaps a swift-sailing Arab felucca, with foreward-slanting masts and triangular sails, had reached Mombasa ahead of the European vessels. The sultan was preparing to destroy these Christian invaders. He went about it in a crafty manner.

A boat came out from the shore, bringing presents of a live sheep and palm-leaf baskets containing oranges, lemons, and sugar. "The sultan welcomes you," said a white-robed official. "If you will bring your vessels into the inner harbor, meat, vegetables, and fruit will be given to you freely."

Gama looked at the inner harbor. He realized that once his ships were inside it, they would find it difficult to leave hurriedly. "We will anchor in this outer harbor," he said.

Later he told his crew, "No one will go ashore tonight. We must keep a most careful watch, for yonder Arabs appear too friendly."

About midnight, two heavy Arab boats were rowed silently toward the ships. Men with daggers strapped to their waists slipped over

the side and began to swim through the starlit water. They reached the little *Berrio* without being seen. Nervous Portuguese seamen heard faint sounds of splashing, but they thought the noise was being made by fish playing on the surface of the water.

Some of the Arabs started cutting the heavy rope cables which in those days were used instead of chains to anchor ships. Others climbed silently up the sides of the *Berrio* and began

slashing through the rigging. The Arabs knew that if the *Berrio* drifted free of her anchors and was unable to raise sail, she would run aground at the entrance to the inner harbor.

A Portuguese officer caught sight of the dark figures on deck. "To arms! To arms!" he roared. "We are attacked!"

On the deck of the *Berrio* seamen and Arabs slashed at one another in the darkness. Torches were lighted hastily and the wicks of iron lanterns turned higher. The Arabs were driven over the side, and their boats disappeared into the darkness.

Gama hoisted sail the next morning and left Mombasa. He steered up the coast, searching for some quiet inlet where he could obtain fresh water. He was also very anxious to find fruits and vegetables. In those days no one knew that fruit and vegetables were a certain cure for scurvy. But Gama had noticed that his men recovered when they ate bananas, oranges, and mangoes, and drank the juice of lemons.

The little *Berrio* had been badly pounded during the Atlantic voyage, so Gama decided to abandon her. Her crew was divided among the other three ships. Then she was set on fire, so that valuable iron might be recovered easily from her charred timbers.

Good fortune brought Gama to the little

town of Malindi, thirty miles north of Mombasa. The old Arab ruler was no friend of the sultan of Mombasa, and he was delighted to hear that Gama also regarded him as an enemy. "You may anchor here safely," he said. "By the head of the Prophet I swear that you will have no trouble in Malindi."

Gama looked closely at the old man. He saw only truth and friendship in the Arab's bearded face. "Yes," he replied. "I will bring my ships into your harbor. We are weary after so long at sea, and we have found no favor among the people farther south."

This time Gama tried to find suitable gifts among the trash aboard the ships. But all he could offer was a blue cloak, a felt hat, some coral necklaces, a couple of enamel basins, and six yards of cheap cloth.

That evening, when Gama went ashore to dine with the Arab prince, he must have felt ashamed of those wretched presents. His host

came to meet him in a beautiful barge of polished mahogany, rowed by Negroes wearing red-and-gold uniforms. A canopy of fine blue material stretched from one end of the barge to the other, and the seats were covered with white-satin cushions. The prince sat amidships on an ebony chair inlaid with a diamond-shaped pattern of pure silver.

Four Arab vessels from India were anchored in the harbor. Gama examined them with in-

terest and excitement. These ships had actually crossed the Indian Ocean, and in their holds were the spices and silks and rare perfumes which Europe longed for.

As friendship grew between the Portuguese and the amiable people of Malindi, Gama questioned the Arab ruler about the voyage to India.

"It is one of no great hardship," the prince told him. "I have heard of your country of Portugal. I can guess how long and dangerous your voyage has been already, for you have come round the southern cape of this land of Africa. What lies ahead of you is much easier. Listen, this is the secret. Every year, from April to September, the wind blows steadily from Africa to India. A vessel from Africa can sail straight before it until India is reached. But from December to February, the wind blows from India to Africa. The same vessel can return safely and without delay to Malindi, or Mombasa, or anywhere else along this coast. That is how our ships make their voyages every year."

"Yet I would like to have with me a man who understands these winds," said Gama. "One, also, who knows the coast of India."

"You are prudent," said the gray-bearded Arab. "The wealthiest part of India is along the coast of Malabar. All our vessels go there to trade in the city of Calicut. But that coast is only 150 miles in length, and you might

miss it altogether. Yes, you must have a wise pilot who knows the coast of Malabar. I will find one for you."

The man the Arab ruler chose was Ahmad Ibn Majid, a sea-browned, elderly man with a fiercely curved nose and dark, farseeing eyes. He was the finest Arab pilot of the Indian Ocean, and his name is still revered today by the Arab navigators of east Africa.

When he came to Gama's cabin, he handled

the European navigation instruments in an expert manner. "The coast of Malabar is treacherous to those who do not know it," he said, "but I can take you to India. This is the month of April. Let us sail with the monsoon—which is what we call these periodic winds—as soon as possible."

Water barrels were filled, sheep were housed on the decks, and the holds were filled with great quantities of good fresh food. On April 24, 1498, the *Sao Gabriel* led the *Sao Rafael* and the *Sao Maria* out of Malindi harbor, and Africa was left astern.

A warm, wet wind was scurrying across the ocean. The sky was pale blue, and the damp air felt like tepid steam.

"Steer northeast," said Ahmad. "The monsoon blows strongly, Captain."

The great white sails swayed outward. The Portuguese ships went pitching across the hissing wave tops, their bowsprits pointing almost directly along the golden reflection of the sunrise.

At Malindi the Portuguese ships had been several hundred miles south of the equator. Now, as they rolled northward across the Indian Ocean, they crossed the equator into the Northern Hemisphere. The sailors saw familiar stars climbing into the sky—the Great Bear, Orion, and the polestar. These were like old friends to the men, and they no longer felt lost and alone in a dark world filled with unknown stars.

Every day that splendid monsoon swept the ships onward to the distant coast of India. On the twenty-sixth day at sea the sailors sighted land through sheets of warm rain.

"Yonder lies India," said Ahmad. "We lie north of Calicut, but when this wind and rain abate, we will swing to the south. That will bring us into the port of Calicut."

On May 20, 1498, Gama wrote in his journal, "This day we came to anchor off the coast of Malabar in India. God be thanked that our outward voyage is done."

Gama and his ships had been at sea for almost eleven months. During that time they had sailed about eight thousand miles. They had fought storms at sea and hostile Arabs on land, and had left their dead in graves in Africa or in the silent depths of the ocean. But Vasco da Gama had fulfilled his mission. His were the first European vessels to reach India.

The open sea rolled to within a few yards of the houses of Calicut. There was no harbor, merely a palm-fringed shore. A mile south of the town flowed a wide river with muddy banks. Ships were anchored in the mouth of this river. Great crocodiles crawled among the stiltlike roots of mangrove trees. Bright-plumaged kingfishers flew low above the water, and white-winged egrets searched eagerly for food in muddy ponds.

A stone wall nine feet high surrounded Calicut. Inside it rose neat houses built of adobe or stone, with high roofs of gray palm thatch. Among the houses grew wide-branched *guli-mohur* or flamboyant trees, covered with masses of scarlet flowers. Blue, green, and golden parakeets squawked and fluttered among the pink blossoms of cassia trees. Hordes of chattering monkeys capered up and down the gray trunks of lofty palms.

The streets of Calicut were winding and narrow. Dark-fronted shops were filled with bales of silk; sacks of cloves, nutmegs, mace, and camphor; and bags of sweet brown cane sugar. In the open-air markets were gathered the fruit sellers. Here one could buy lemons, oranges, mangoes, bananas, and many strange fruits, all of them piled high on wickerwork trays.

All the races of Asia seemed to be strolling along the streets of Calicut. Round-faced Chinese with heavy pigtails mingled with fat, ivory-skinned Turks. There were tall and slender Somali tribesmen from Africa, clad in white robes and wearing heavy silver bracelets on their dusky wrists. There were quick-moving little Malays; Arabs in flowing robes and green turbans; pale-skinned, black-haired Syrians; brightly dressed Brahmans; and people from all over India.

The next morning Gama sent for Joao Nunes, the seaman who could speak Hebrew and Arabic.

"Go ashore and find out what you can," he ordered. "Be back on the ship at sunset."

Nunes returned that evening with plenty of news. "This great town of Calicut is ruled by a prince called the zamorin," he reported. "He is away at present but will return within a few days. All the trade of the coast seems to

be in the hands of the Arabs. They are jealous of our arrival here. A group of them greeted me with the words, 'May the devil fly away with you!' These Arabs will give us trouble, my lord Captain General."

Nunes then went on to describe the wonders he had seen that day. "All the ships of Portugal would not be sufficient to carry the cargoes we could obtain in this city. All Europe would buy the spices, silks, perfumes, silverwork, and jewels I have seen ashore."

When the zamorin returned to Calicut, he sent a message that he wished to see the commander of the European ships. Gama went ashore and was borne through the crowded, noisy streets on a handsome wooden litter covered with a fine silk canopy. Behind him tramped twelve of his strongest and most reliable men, armed with swords and daggers.

The zamorin's palace was a low, white-walled building surrounded by a fragrant garden filled with flowering shrubs set in smooth green lawns. Gama passed through shady halls and chambers filled with the perfume of flowers and incense, until he reached the royal apartments.

When Gama entered the royal chamber, the zamorin was reclining on a silken couch. He was a slender, handsome man of about forty, with a sharp-featured face that was grave and thoughtful. He wore loose silken pants which hung gracefully from his waist to his ankles. The upper half of his body was bare, but on his brown chest dangled rich ornaments of gold. His lean and sinewy arms were decorated with broad golden bangles.

The Indian ruler gazed curiously at Vasco da Gama. He saw a man whose countenance, darkened by tropical suns, was as hard and as strong-willed as his own. "Why have you come to Calicut?" he asked. "Of what nation are you?"

"Portugal has been seeking a sea passage to India for almost a hundred years," Gama replied through an interpreter. "We are the first to find it. Let me describe our country to you, O Prince."

The interview was a friendly one. The zamorin listened carefully to everything that Gama told him. At the end of an hour's conversation he said, "Stay ashore tonight. I will order supplies of food and drinking water to be sent out to your ships at once. You and your twelve men will stay in lodgings in the town."

Through the crowded town went Gama and his men, followed by inquisitive eyes. The Portuguese gazed at strange temples and monstrous gilded figures of unknown heathen gods. They eyed greedily the bales of silk and the diamonds lying on jewelers' trays.

The Arab traders of Calicut were furiously jealous of the Portuguese. For centuries they had traded between Africa and India without any interference from European nations. They had grown rich, built fine houses for themselves, and become important people on the coast of Malabar. They saw that the arrival of the Portuguese ships might end their monopoly of trade. They drew softly round the zamorin and started whispering in his ear.

"Choose your friends where you wish, O Prince," said one, "but we beg you to remember that Calicut has grown rich on the trade we Arabs have built up."

"True," added another Arab. "Will the Portuguese do as much to help your city as we have done, O great and wise ruler?"

"Our ships have brought news of what these Portuguese did in east Africa," murmured a third. "Beware, O Zamorin, lest they destroy Calicut with their accursed guns."

The next day news reached these Arabs that Gama had tried to offer the zamorin absurd gifts: four strings of coral beads, six hats, four scarlet hoods, twelve pieces of striped cotton, two cases of honey, one case of sugar, two cases of olive oil, and six washbasins. Perhaps, poor man, he had nothing better to give. But the offering of these miserable gifts to the wealthy zamorin of Calicut was one of Gama's worst mistakes.

"The least of us merchants would bring more costly gifts than those," sneered the Arabs gathered round the zamorin. "Now you can see for yourself what poor creatures these Europeans are. Think well, O Zamorin. We Arabs can move to other countries in India or elsewhere and start business again. But this is your country and your city. You cannot go elsewhere. Will you withdraw your friendship from us and give it to these miserable and bloodthirsty Christians?"

The zamorin began to turn against Gama. The Arabs encouraged the population of Cali-

cut to insult the Portuguese seamen strolling through the streets. Knives were drawn, clubs were swung, and blood was spilled.

Gama could manage a mutinous crew or a ship tossing crazily in a wild tempest, but he did not know how to deal with the zamorin and the Arabs. He lost his temper and started making threats. His threats were backed up by Portuguese swords and the black muzzles of his ships' cannons. The zamorin, seeing how badly things were going, tried to deal with the Portuguese in a fair manner. But he was powerless to turn aside the Arabs' cold and deadly hatred of the Portuguese explorers.

On August 29, 1498, Gama ordered the return voyage to Portugal to begin. "I will come back," he threatened the zamorin's officers. "There will be more ships next time, and larger ones. My cannons will repay the insults and evil treatment I have received."

The enraged Arabs of Calicut made a last effort to destroy Gama and his ships. As the Portuguese sailed out of the river's mouth, they were surrounded and attacked by about seventy large ships filled with armed men.

This was a situation Gama knew how to deal with. "Load and stand by your guns," he ordered. "Aim at the nearest boats, but do not fire until I give the command."

The speeding Arab boats drew to within a hundred yards of the onward-gliding boats.

"Fire!" said Captain Vasco da Gama.

The Portuguese vessels continued to move seaward. Behind them they left broken and sinking boats, wounded men struggling in the water, and black-finned sharks closing in on patches of blood-reddened water. Such was the Portuguese farewell to this newly discovered land of India.

Gama had sailed from India at the wrong

time of the year. The monsoon from Africa was still blowing. For weeks his three ships struggled to make headway. They ran short of fresh food, and the drinking water became slimy and foul. Scurvy broke out again, and the bodies of thirty men were dropped over the side. The survivors were so weak that they could scarcely manage to sail the ships.

"Only death awaits us ahead," the officers declared at a meeting in Gama's cabin. "Let us turn back to India, Captain, while some of us yet remain alive."

Gama nodded. He, too, was in despair. "Should the wind continue to blow steadily from Africa," he said, "we will turn back tomorrow night."

The wind changed the next morning. Now the ships went swiftly ahead, rising and falling across the spray-feathered wave tops.

They sighted Malindi on January 7, 1499, more than four months after leaving Calicut.

The friendly chieftain gave them a kindly welcome. Thin-bodied, sickly Portuguese reached out gratefully for the baskets of fruit, eggs, vegetables, and coconuts which were brought aboard. For the next five days they ate and drank as much as they could, until scurvy gradually disappeared.

Down the coast went the three ships, pausing only to pick up water, fresh food, and firewood in lonely villages. More than sixty men had died since leaving Portugal. Not enough seamen were left to handle all three ships, and Gama decided that one of them would have to be abandoned.

The 200-ton *Sao Rafael* was beached and her cargo stowed aboard the two remaining ships. It was then set on fire and utterly destroyed.

Around the Cape of Good Hope went the two ships in a fine, hurrying breeze. Fever-sick men shivered in the cold winds of the south Atlantic, but those same winds blew northward day after day. Gama held a straight and steady course from the tip of South Africa to the Cape Verde Islands. There the ships anchored for a few days. Gama's gentle brother Paulo, suffering from tuberculosis, was taken ashore. He died on the second day. With Paulo's death Gama lost his best—and one of his few—real friends. He also lost a very valuable aide. Paulo had never made a mistake during the whole voyage. He had cared for his sickly and frightened crew and had been one of the very few Portuguese who had managed to remain friends with the people of Calicut.

Two tired little ships, with weather-whitened cordage and blistered paint, came creeping up the Tagus River early in September, 1499. Aboard were about 70 lean and shabby men, all who remained of the 150 seamen who had sailed two years before.

The entire population, except the families of the men who had died, rejoiced over their return, and the church bells rang. Gama had found the sea route to India, and times of great prosperity now awaited Portugal. He had brought back samples of the rare products which Malabar could supply in endless quantities. And then there was east Africa as well. Portuguese ships would be able to take Negro slaves, ivory, raw gold, and other commodities to India. Portugal could build a new empire in east Africa, and perhaps another empire in India. King Manuel was overwhelmed with delight at Gama's success.

While the rest of Europe watched jealously, Portugal prepared a new and stronger fleet for a second voyage to India. But Gama was weary with seafaring for the time being. He wanted to rest in the sunny countryside of Portugal, to enjoy fresh food and good wine, and to sleep in a comfortable bed at night. He had money enough now, for the king had given him a pension for life. During his long residence ashore, Vasco da Gama, at the age of forty, married Catharina de Athayde, an elegant young girl of noble family.

Thirteen vessels sailed for India under the command of Pedro Cabral. The Arabs were waiting for them in Calicut, and soon after the ships reached Malabar, forty-four Portuguese were killed by an angry mob. Cabral, a tough and brutal man, turned his guns on the town. Half of Calicut was knocked into ruins. The Portuguese vessels then sailed 150 miles down the coast to the port of Cochin. The ruler of this town was an enemy of the zamorin. He welcomed the arrival of the Portuguese. Cabral's ships returned to Lisbon with cargoes of cinnamon, pepper, cloves, musk, and Chinese silks. Although six ships were lost, Portugal made 100 per cent net profit on this voyage.

When the fleet returned to Portugal, however, King Manuel and Pedro Cabral had some kind of disagreement. The king, in a temper, sent for Gama. "I want you to take command of the next expedition to India," he said. "You will have twenty ships in your fleet, Captain—ten to carry cargoes from India, five to cruise in the Indian Ocean and destroy Arab shipping, and five to remain on the east

African coast and guard our new settlements there."

Vasco da Gama had a dark side to his nature. He could never forget a grievance, and the violence of his temper sometimes caused his own officers to tremble. Perhaps the new title given him by the king—Admiral of the Indian Seas—made him conceited. Whatever the reason, he began to behave in a most savage manner. His ships sailed along the east African coast, punishing local native rulers and attacking Arab vessels. Setting course across the Indian Ocean, Gama reached Calicut in October, 1502.

The zamorin realized his mistake in having made an enemy of the Portuguese. He sent a message to Gama, offering his friendship.

"Deport every Arab in Calicut, and you may have time to save your city," Gama replied.

The zamorin hesitated. The Portuguese

demand was almost impossible to satisfy. The big ships swung in closer to the town, and their guns roared. Tall white houses, Indian temples, and warehouses collapsed among a tangle of splintered trees.

"I warned them that I would return," said Gama to his men. "Now sail south to Cochin, where the population was wise enough to make friends with us."

Great cargoes of spices were awaiting the Portuguese ships at Cochin. The vessels were almost fully laden when another message from the zamorin reached Gama. "I implore you to return to Calicut," wrote the prince. "We will sign a treaty of peace and commerce as soon as you wish. I see now that the Portuguese could become powerful friends."

The letter was a trap, and Gama fell into that trap. He sailed for Calicut in his ship, the *Flor de la Mar* (Ocean Flower), accompanied by a little vessel of about forty tons.

Small, fast-sailing Arab ships were waiting in the darkness of the night. They ringed round the *Flor de la Mar* and opened fire with every gun they could aim at the Portuguese ships. Hordes of Arab fighting men swung themselves by ropes onto the deck of Gama's ship. In mad rage they swarmed all over it, swinging heavy, razor-edged scimitars which could cut a man in half with a single blow.

Gama nearly died that night. By sheer luck,

three other Portuguese ships caught sight of the flaring torches and heard the noise of battle. They came swiftly to the help of their admiral, and drove the Arabs off.

"This is the zamorin's work," said Gama, eyeing the dead Portuguese and Arabs on the deck. "Now he shall pay for it."

With every ship he could obtain, Gama sailed for Calicut. Arab ships came out to meet him, but they were driven off, and Calicut was bombarded again. When Gama sailed away, most of the city lay in ruins.

Westward around the Cape of Good Hope went the ships. Once again the Portuguese sailors shivered in great tempests of rain and wind and freezing blasts of hail and snow. Thankfully they bore northward again toward the summer seas of the equator and reached Lisbon on October 11, 1503.

So ended Admiral Vasco da Gama's second voyage. He had founded Portuguese trading posts in east Africa and also along the coast of India. He had filled his ships with cargoes which brought new wealth to Portugal. But he had made thousands of relentless enemies for his country. The Arabs of Calicut and east Africa, Arabia and north Africa, now hated the Portuguese in a deadly and unforgiving manner.

Ten years after Gama had discovered the route to India, the east African coast from Sofala to Lamu had become an empire for the Portuguese. Ports, churches, and handsome stone houses were arising among the groves of palm trees. In India, Portuguese trading posts dotted the coast from Cochin to Goa, a distance of 500 miles. While Vasco da Gama, now a wealthy landlord in Portugal, went on squabbling with his king about a title, a larger pension, and a larger estate for himself, the Portuguese empire grew larger

and more prosperous. But trouble was already coming to Portugal.

"Why should we plow poor soil and weed our stony ground?" the simple Portuguese countrymen asked one another. "Our friends who went to India and Africa are now living like princes. They have Negro servants to wait on them and Negro workers to care for their fine new estates, while here we live in poverty."

The men of Portugal began to leave their country. Around the Cape of Good Hope they went and onward to Mombasa, Malindi, or Sofala; Goa, Cochin, or Cannanore. Some died of fever or heatstroke or scurvy, but most of them prospered as they never could have prospered in Portugal. Only a few of these men ever returned.

Now the fields of Portugal lay untilled in the hot sunshine. Fences rotted away, and lean cattle roamed across acres covered only with weeds and rank grass. Wheat became scarce and was soon worth its weight in silver. Vegetables and supplies of meat almost disappeared. Famine struck Portugal. While the city of Lisbon grew in luxury and splendor, the population became desperately hungry. Men died of starvation while the wharves of the Tagus River were piled with costly imports from India and Africa.

Hatred of Portugal continued to rise among the natives of Africa and India. The officials sent out to administer the Portuguese empire were lazy and dishonest. They made no effort to win the friendship of the races they governed. Only the poor settlers lived in peace and happiness with their Arab and Negro neighbors in Africa. They managed their farms, treated their workers kindly, and sometimes married off their grown-up sons to handsome Arab or Swahili girls. But the Portuguese empire began to crumble in Gama's own lifetime, and ruthless natives swept down from Arabia to attack the coastal towns of Malindi, Sofala, and Mombasa.

During this period King Manuel died, and his son John ascended the throne of Portugal. King John III realized what was happening in India and Africa. In 1524 he sent for Gama and begged him to serve Portugal again.

"Restore good order to our settlements," he pleaded. "Send home our useless army leaders, and imprison our dishonest officials. I now create you Viceroy of India, with unlimited powers to reward and punish. Make sure, I pray you, that our settlements in India are preserved. Try also to restore efficiency to our settlements in Africa. We need those ports for our fleets voyaging to and from India."

Gama was over sixty years of age. He had a family of six children, some of whom were grown-up. He was a great and wealthy man in his own country, and he owned the title of Count of Vidigueira, a title his descendants

still hold today. Yet he could not resist the temptation to return to the countries he had discovered twenty-five years before.

"I serve Portugal to the end," he said. "I will leave at once, Your Majesty."

Gama sailed on his third voyage in April, 1524. He reached India in September.

Corrupt Portuguese officials tried to run away when they heard that the dreaded old Vasco da Gama was returning. A few escaped, but others soon found themselves in jail. From morning to night, six days a week, Gama tried to bring back justice and prosperity to the Portuguese settlements. He punished and he rewarded. He sailed from port to port, dismissing crooked administrators and threatening surly native rulers. Greedy little civil servants, narrow-minded and without loyalty to their country, conspired to prevent Gama from discovering how bad conditions really were in India.

All this unending work was too much for Vasco da Gama. The glaring sun of India, the ceaseless, whining mosquitoes, the polluted water, and the endless hours in stuffy offices destroyed his failing strength.

Gama felt death approaching, but he would not rest quietly at home. "Evil weeds grow too thickly in this fair garden of India," he said. "I must finish plucking them out before the sun goes down."

He spent his last few days still trying to fulfill the royal orders he had been given in Portugal. On December 24, 1524, he died in Cochin. (Thirteen years later his coffin was brought back to Portugal.)

Perhaps before he died, Vasco da Gama bitterly regretted the mistakes he had made in his days of exploration. He may have realized that he had created too many enemies for his little country throughout Africa and India. Those who came after him, however, were no wiser and a great deal less honest.

The Portuguese empire in Africa gradually disappeared. Stone quays crumbled into the warm salt water, and harbors filled with sand. Wild animals roamed among fire-blackened houses and the broken buildings of deserted farms, forts, and warehouses. The jungle came back to cover up the traces of a short-lived and utterly decayed empire.